Original title:
Mossy Metaphors

Copyright © 2025 Creative Arts Management OÜ
All rights reserved.

Author: Thomas Sinclair
ISBN HARDBACK: 978-1-80566-731-5
ISBN PAPERBACK: 978-1-80566-860-2

The Heart of the Hidden Forest

In shadows deep, the squirrels prance,
With acorns tossed, they start a dance.
A hedgehog grins with a cheeky wink,
While mushrooms giggle, just think, oh think!

A deer in a hat sips morning dew,
Claims it's a tea brewed just for two.
With every rustle, secrets spill,
The trees can't help but laugh at will.

Through tangled roots and vines so sly,
The fireflies strike a pose, oh my!
A lizard rehearses its grand ballet,
While frogs compose a croaky play.

The forest hums a silly tune,
As raccoons juggle by the moon.
Each creature's voice adds to the cheer,
In this merry land, there's nothing to fear.

Resting Under the Whispering Sky

Beneath the clouds, a snail takes naps,
Dreaming of cheese and fuzzy traps.
A bunny wears a giant hat,
Pretends to be a wise old cat.

The sunbeams dance on the grass so green,
While ladybugs strut like they're on the scene.
A butterfly farts, it's quite the feat,
Sending giggles to the ants on their feet.

Daffodils chuckle as they bloom,
Hummingbirds zoom with a little vroom.
A worm tells jokes from deep underground,
While daisies sway, laughter all around.

The skies burst forth in colors bright,
As everyone joins in the silly flight.
Nature's comedy is always near,
In this whimsical world, let's spread some cheer!

Under Foot

Beneath my shoes, a jungle thrives,
A footpath paved with tiny lives.
Sneaky friends, they squish and squirm,
While I just dance and wiggle my term.

I step on court jesters, they laugh and cheer,
Their leafy tricks, oh, they are dear.
With every stomp, a party starts,
Nature's groove plays on my parts.

a Whispered Tale

In a forest where laughter hides,
A tale unfolds, like wiggly slides.
The trees gossip, what a lively crew,
Telling secrets to me and you.

Blades of grass take a bow each time,
They're the chorus, make the joke rhyme.
A squirrel chuckles, a puffy-cheeked sprite,
While ants form a line just to join in the fight.

Back to the Roots

Let's dig deep, find the trunk of fun,
Where roots are tangled, and jokes are spun.
A worm winks at a beetle so spry,
"Why did the chicken? Oh, pass it by!"

In the soil, we share our dreams,
With puns and giggles, we sprout our schemes.
There's wisdom hidden in every groove,
Nature's punchline helps us move.

In the Company of Green

Amidst the ferns and dandelion fluff,
A party brews, but is it too tough?
The grass blades sway, it's a dancing spree,
To the funky beat from a bumblebee.

Mushrooms wear hats, oh what a sight,
With polka dots dancing in the light.
Together we bumble, giggle, and sway,
In the company of green, we laugh all day.

Grains of Time in the Slumbering Earth

In the earth's embrace, whispers grow deep,
Grains of time, they never sleep.
Each pebble and twig tells a funny story,
Of shadows that dance in fleeting glory.

The past tickles roots with glee,
As snails slide by with jokes to see.
In the silence, we find our cheer,
With nature's humor ringing clear.

Nature's Gentle Kinship

A squirrel stole my sandwich bite,
He chattered with delight.
The trees giggled in the breeze,
Their whispers tickle, aiming to tease.

The daisies wore their best sun hats,
While ants marched like tiny spats.
A butterfly danced, so spry,
Turning heads as it fluttered by.

Rabbits hop in comedic flops,
While tadpoles slide and flip, then stop.
Nature's jesters, with glee do play,
In their delightful, wild ballet.

As dusk falls, the crickets sing,
A chorus to end this funny fling.
With stars as our audience above,
Nature laughs, and we feel its love.

The Weight of a Thousand Leaves

A leaf fell softly on my head,
I swore it whispered, 'Get out of bed!'
A squirrel chuckled, threw acorns galore,
As if my morning needed more.

The branches bowed, they moaned with flair,
'Our weight is much more than you could bear!'
I laughed so hard, I nearly fell,
Nature's jesters know how to tell.

A pile of leaves, a mountain so grand,
Time for the critters' joyful band.
Rabbits dive in, creating a scene,
Wreaking havoc of the vibrant green.

So next time you stroll beneath the trees,
Watch for whispers in the breeze.
For laughter lives in every green,
In nature's show, we're all unseen.

Enigmas of the Ancients

Mossy rocks like olden minds,
Guarding secrets, a riddle finds.
An owl hoots like it holds a joke,
Wisdom wrapped in a fluffy cloak.

The stones smirk beneath the haze,
As if they know our silly phase.
'Where do birds go when they nap?'
A question that could warp a map.

Frogs croak tales of lands unseen,
In ancient tongues, a playful sheen.
The shadows shuffle, wriggling tight,
Trading puns in the low moonlight.

So ponder not just the trees' old tales,
But giggles hidden in their scales.
For humor is nature's special prize,
In every nook, it slyly lies.

A Tapestry of Earth and Sky

The clouds wore sweaters of fluffy white,
Tickling the sun, pure delight.
Rain drops bounced like playful kids,
Splashing joy on the nearest lids.

The ground chuckled, covered in blooms,
Each petal a clumsy, sweet perfume.
Bees danced hard, caught in mid-flight,
Their buzzing giggles, oh what a sight!

The mountains snickered, proud and loud,
'We've seen the funkiest of the crowd.'
While rivers twirled in gleeful loops,
As nature's jam turned up the troops.

So linger here, where laughs abound,
In nature's realm, joy can be found.
With every breath, the world's a play,
Painted in laughter, come what may.

The Language of Damp Earth

In a world where moisture thrives,
Words sprout like little hives.
Each syllable a leaf of cheer,
Giggling whispers that we hear.

Slippery sentences glide with grace,
Tickling toes in the wet embrace.
Puns take root beneath the gloom,
And laughter grows in every room.

Treading on a Carpet of Green

Each step a squish, a joyful squeal,
Underfoot, the softest feel.
Bouncing giggles with every tread,
Worms join in, no tears to shed.

A fungal fanfare, wild and bright,
Beneath our feet, they wiggle tight.
Who knew that walking could be so fun?
A silly romp under the sun.

Shadows Dance in Ferns

In the shade, where secrets sway,
Ferns perform their cabaret.
With every breeze, they twirl and spin,
Chasing giggles wrapped in green.

Laughter stirs the leafy ground,
As hidden critters scurry 'round.
They plot their pranks with clever flair,
Beneath the ferns, a jester's lair.

The Poetry of Silent Growth

Underneath, where roots converse,
They weave a tale, a universe.
Slow and steady, they won't rush,
Sneaking rhymes in every hush.

Time slips by in stealthy shoes,
While nature pens its vibrant muse.
A giggle here, a chuckle there,
Whispers rise in fragrant air.

Glistening Pathways in the Fog

In the mist, the path does gleam,
A twisty road, like a bad dream.
With puddles laughing, they tease my shoes,
As I dance with raindrops, I can't refuse.

A squirrel winks, he's quite the sight,
His acorn stash, a treasure tight.
He hosts a party with mushrooms wide,
While I just stumble, trying to hide.

The daisies gossip, whispering cheer,
About the chap who tripped with fear.
As I pass by with a goofy grin,
Maybe next time, I'll just hop in!

Through shafts of light, the glimmers play,
Where shadows prance in a silly ballet.
I'll name this dance, the 'Oops and Whee!'
Who knew fog could be so free?

The Melodies of Muffled Steps

Soft whispers float on the ground,
Shuffling feet, here and around.
A frog croaks out a tune so loud,
While crickets chirp, they're quite proud.

My sneakers squeak, a comical sound,
In harmony with nature all around.
A tune of twirls and little hops,
The woodland's rhythm never stops.

Leaves clap softly, a gentle cheer,
As my attempts to dance bring sneers.
But owls just hoot, they seem to know,
This waltz of laughs is quite the show.

Each step I take, a catchy beat,
The forest jig is pretty sweet.
I'll keep on moving, with all my glee,
To the sound of nature's symphony.

Fables in the Foliage

In leafy tales, where critters play,
A fox spins stories, quite the display.
With a hat of leaves, he takes the stage,
Telling jokes that are all the rage.

A rabbit munches, ears in tune,
He hops along, a furry cartoon.
The bushes giggle, they rustle with glee,
Every punchline is under a tree.

Lizards gossip, with tails that flick,
Swaying to stories, their favorite trick.
They've got the scoop on the owl's last snack,
And secrets dwell deep in the green backpack.

When twilight falls, and stars shine bright,
The fables linger, a cozy sight.
In the foliage, laughter reigns supreme,
Nature's own chat, a joyful dream.

The Fabric of Forgotten Steps

In the quiet woods, steps once taken,
Echo softly, like hearts that are shaken.
Dusty trails and stories weave,
Of funny moments, you wouldn't believe.

A canvas of leaves, painted in hues,
Recalls the day that cricket snooze.
With tangled roots, I trip and laugh,
While a turtle films, my silly gaffe.

The whispers of giants, a breeze so light,
Carry tales of mischief through the night.
Their roots entwined, as if to say,
"Keep dancing, darling, you're okay!"

Each footprint holds a chuckle, a cheer,
As I roam these paths, year after year.
The fabric of life, so rich and bright,
In every step, pure delight!

Beneath the Canopy's Embrace

Under leaves, a secret chat,
Squirrels discuss, 'Is that a cat?'
Branches sway, they shrug and tease,
Nature's gossip in the breeze.

Beneath the green, a wise old frog,
Thinks he's king among the bog.
With every croak, he drops a pun,
His court of bugs is always fun.

Dappled sunlight plays peek-a-boo,
Dance of shadows, quite the view.
Fungi laugh and twirl around,
In this kingdom, joy is found.

Roots intertwine like friends at play,
Nearby a snail takes all day.
In this forest party, all are hip,
Even the trees sway and slip!

Tangled Thoughts in Nature's Cradle

A spider spins a web of dreams,
While ants construct their tiny beams.
Each thread a tale, each path a joke,
In this grove, life's a playful poke.

A butterfly flits, all flouncy and bright,
Whispers to flowers, 'You smell just right!'
They giggle and blush, such vibrant chatter,
In nature's realm, all's a bit madder.

Underneath ferns, the raccoons brawl,
Playing tag as they trip and fall.
With a splash, they dive in the creek,
Nature's jesters, never meek.

Owls hoot wise, but miss the fun,
While doves complain, 'We need to run!'
In tangled thoughts, they find their score,
With laughter echoing evermore.

The Softness of Time

Time flows gently, like a stream,
Whispers secrets, lives a dream.
Moss cushions all that wobbles near,
A tickle of green, a chuckle clear.

Old stones chuckle, wear a grin,
Holding stories of where they've been.
A raccoon stops, gives a wink,
'Let's not rush, let's just think!'

Sunshine giggles, dances low,
As shadows stretch and say hello.
Butterflies pause for a sweet snack,
In this soft place, we lose the track.

Time seems silly, like a clown,
Dancing quickly, then settling down.
With each heartbeat, joy and glee,
In nature's arms, we'd all agree.

Verdant Veils of Memory

A tapestry of green unfurls,
Each leaf a tale, as life swirls.
Crickets chirp, spin yarns and songs,
In this place, where laughter belongs.

Mushrooms chuckle, 'We're not just food!'
While squirrels leap in playful mood.
The trees listen, roots entwine tight,
Caught in the thrill of a leafy flight.

Memories dance on beams of gold,
Whispering secrets of tales retold.
A lost sock smells of flowers bright,
In this green realm, all feels right.

Wanderers laugh, trip on their feet,
While talking stones share rhymes so sweet.
Life's a jest beneath the trees,
Where verdant veils bring us to our knees.

The Green Murmurs of the Earth

In the forest, giggles rise,
Little greens with clever eyes.
They tickle roots and tease the stones,
Whispering secrets in hushed tones.

Fungi dance with topsy glee,
While crickets strum a symphony.
The grass performs a stand-up show,
Mosses laugh, they're in the know.

Every leaf a jokester bold,
Bouncing tales of times of old.
With roots that twist in playful jest,
They craft a stage and never rest.

So tiptoe through this verdant mirth,
Join the laughs that fill the earth.
For in these woods, the funny thrives,
In every nook, the joy survives.

Whispers of Life in Silent Spaces

In quiet nooks where shadows dwell,
Tiny whispers weave a spell.
The toadstools wink, a secret pact,
Among the ferns, they laugh intact.

Crickets chirp a witty tune,
As squirrels mock beneath the moon.
Old logs stand like jokers wise,
Ever waiting for surprise.

A beetle rolls his tiny ball,
While others gather for the call.
In twinkling light, they play and prance,
Nature's jesters in a trance.

So come and pause, delight in jest,
In silent spaces, life's at best.
These whispers cheer with every breath,
In shadows deep, there's humor, yet.

Serenity in the Shadows

Underneath the leafy shade,
Lies a world where jokes are made.
Each shadow holds a playful grin,
As nature plays her violin.

The mushrooms boast their heads so round,
In the quiet, laughter's found.
A playful breeze makes branches sway,
While ants engage in a grand display.

A sleepy owl begins to snore,
Echoing through vines galore.
Around the trunk, a dance unfolds,
Where every creature's story's told.

So nestle down where shadows twine,
Find the peace in puns divine.
Among the leaves, let laughter flow,
In serenity's embrace, we'll glow.

The Embrace of Ancient Growth

In tangled roots, the old ones sing,
Each knot and twist a funny thing.
With every ring of age they boast,
They whisper tales we love the most.

Up high, the branches sway and twist,
Crafting plays that can't be missed.
The wind, a roguish jester's breath,
Brings life alive, defying death.

Each gnarled trunk a comic tale,
With quirky quirks that never fail.
And in their leaves, a giggle hides,
In ancient growth, true joy abides.

So wander deep where past meets play,
Let nature's humor light your way.
In every grove, in every bend,
The embrace of growth, a laughter's friend.

Layers of Life in Subdued Glow

Beneath the shade, the stories creep,
Like turtles racing in a quiet sweep.
With every step, a squishy cheer,
Nature's jokes tickle, oh so near.

A blanket green with whispers bold,
Puns await between stories told.
In tangled roots, a dance unfolds,
Mischief whispers in tones of gold.

Each pebble's laugh, a gentle tease,
In the woodland's arms, nobody sees.
Light filters down with a giggling sigh,
As squirrels wink and critters fly.

Here in the calm, the humor thrums,
With every poke, a laughter comes.
We're just layers, as life spills on,
Beneath the tranquil, the world moves on.

Echoes of the Underfoot

Where feet patter on the silent ground,
The giggles of roots are all around.
Each footfall lands with a silly plop,
And shy mushrooms rise up to swap.

The squeak of grass holds a secret grin,
While ants march home, their tails tucked in.
Sticky situations? They're so quite fair,
In the field of jokes, it's always rare.

Pebbles chuckle, making puns on toes,
While sprouts stretch upward, in silly throes.
The world below, a comedic play,
Where every tiptoe leads to a fray.

With echoes mixed in laughter's glee,
The soil hums tunes of jubilee.
In every rustle, a joke appears,
At the underfoot, it's fun, not fears.

Where Gray Meets Verdant Dreams

Gray stones chuckle at the emerald spree,
As lively greens laugh, "Come here, just see!"
With every sprout dressed in morning dew,
Nature crafts giggles, fresh as a brew.

In tangled vines, where wild things play,
The laughter grows bold, in whimsical sway.
Mixing hues like a painter's brush,
With winks exchanged, there's never a rush.

A snail slips by with a snail's slow jest,
While foxgloves sway with grace at their best.
Roots dive deep, but dance above ground,
In this banquet of humor, joy is profound.

Between grays and greens, the fun unfolds,
In nature's embrace, laughter never grows old.
So stroll right through, let your heart scheme,
For life's just a play in a verdant dream.

Hushed Conversations with Hills

The hills whisper secrets, hush but keen,
While bushes wiggle in a vibrant green.
Each stone sits, grinning in its seat,
As the breeze tells tales of the day's repeat.

With every rustle, a giggle peeks,
In the harmony of wild, the humor leaks.
Fluffy clouds join in, a merry troupe,
Floating above in a jovial loop.

Crisp leaves jibe at a squirrel's misstep,
Slipping on acorns, oh what a rep!
The trees converse in hushed tones of fun,
While shadows wander, chasing the sun.

In the arms of hills, life softly jests,
With nature's rhythm, it's all the best.
So gather round, let the laughter spill,
In the tender green arms of the playful hill.

Whispers of Green Dreams

In a forest where giggles grow,
Fungi gossip in a merry row.
Leaves wear hats, quite dapper and spry,
While acorns plot to dance and fly.

The squirrels strut with nutty flair,
Chasing each other without a care.
They must think they're in a parade,
While branches cheer in leafy charade.

Sunbeams tickle the woodland floor,
As shadows laugh and hungry snore.
Who knew nature had such a jest?
A world where silliness is the best!

Whispers float on a breezy spree,
Unveiling secrets, wild and free.
In this realm, the ordinary plays,
Skipping through life in curious ways.

Beneath the Canopy's Embrace

Under layers of leafy cheer,
The mushrooms chuckle, far and near.
Rabbits trade jokes with the old oak,
While bees buzz laughs with every stroke.

A raccoon dons a mask of delight,
Sneaking snacks when it's dark at night.
While fireflies wink in playful tease,
Dancing around like confetti leaves.

Twirling vines whisper secrets sly,
Where frogs croak out a lullaby.
Nature's comedians, never so tame,
In this green stage, they play their game.

Every rustle shares a funny tale,
Where laughter echoed in every gale.
Here in the shade, with the trees' embrace,
Life's a comedy, a merry place!

Shadows of Nature's Lullaby

Crouched in the thicket, a snail sings low,
"Time grinds to a halt, watch me go slow!"
While crickets make symphonies with flair,
In the twilight air, they float without care.

The hedgehog juggles fallen leaves,
Crafting art with what autumn weaves.
While sleepy birds hold a feathered show,
With dreams of skyward fame they bestow.

Beneath the stars, the best jokes wait,
As owls hoot punchlines, oh, isn't it great?
Each rustling bush tells a tale to tell,
Where giggles echo in the night's spell.

In shadows deep, where secrets convene,
Nature winks as the world turns green.
And in such laughter, peace takes flight,
In this nocturnal, whimsical night!

The Velvet Cloak of Silence

Draped in silence, the forest sighs,
Turtles tell tales, oh what a surprise!
Snakes slither round as if in a race,
While hedgehogs share puns in their cozy space.

The wind carries whispers of cheesy quips,
With fluttering leaves and chipmunk slips.
"Who stepped on my tail?" a lizard cries,
As shadows chuckle, covering their eyes.

Under branches where the laughter hides,
Frogs leap and hop, like wild joyrides.
In soft darkness, where goofy unfolds,
Nature's silliness, a treasure of old.

With each heartbeat of the night's soft dress,
Fun flourishes wild, a leafy excess.
In this cloak of stillness, the gags take flight,
Painting the dark in a whimsical light!

In the Stillness Between

In the shade where giggles grow,
A squirrel juggles acorns, you know.
The sun peeks through with a wink,
While leaves dance and start to think.

Frogs wear crowns of secret glee,
Making calls to the honeybee.
A snail slides in with a smug little grin,
He knows he's winning, where to begin!

The stream chuckles, tickles the rocks,
While nature eavesdrops, checking the clocks.
A rabbit hops past, with style and flair,
Waving to ferns with extravagant hair!

In this realm of lush delight,
Even shadows are bouncing tight.
With each quirky giggle and twist,
A little more joy we can't resist.

Nurtured by the Earth

Beneath the soil where whispers play,
Worms throw parties every day.
They dance in spirals, twinkle and twist,
While ants waltz past, not one gets missed.

Mushrooms sport hats; oh, what a sight!
Telling secrets to stars at night.
A ladybug prances, all dressed up fine,
In a polka-dot dress, she's one of a kind!

The grasses gossip, trading a joke,
As daisies giggle, no need for smoke.
They whisper to daisies, joining the spree,
In this earthy carnival, wild and free.

The Calm Beneath the Canopy

Beneath the leaves, a choir sings,
Of wriggly worms and funny things.
The breeze is giggling through the trees,
While ants march in synchronized Z's.

A spider spins tales on a silky line,
Crafting a web that's simply divine.
A butterfly flutters, a flamboyant sight,
Wearing stripes, oh what a delight!

The bird with a beak so stylish and neat,
Dances on branches to a heart-pumping beat.
Nature's rhythm, a quirky affair,
Leaves whispering secrets, love in the air.

Time Worn Patterns of Green

In corners where moss weaves its tale,
Lizards brag about their scale.
Each wrinkle and ridge tells a joke,
While shadows peek like an old wise folk.

Pebbles chuckle, covered in grime,
Old as stories, stuck in time.
Every patch a laugh, a tickle, a tease,
Nature's rascals laughing with ease.

Brambles wear crowns, quite proud and spry,
Waving to clouds when they float by.
In this vibrant mess, joy grows free,
In patterns of humor, wait and see!

The Lure of the Enigmatic Trail

With shoes that squeak on forest paths,
A raccoon stares, and then it laughs.
We wander wide on this strange spree,
Where twigs become the symphony.

Each tree's a jester, dressed in green,
Its bark tells tales we've never seen.
I trip on roots, and oh, how I spin,
While squirrels gather, wearing a grin.

A Reverie in Shaded Hues

Sunlight peeks like a playful tease,
Painting the ground with a gentle breeze.
A butterfly flits, in search of delight,
While I chase shadows that dance in flight.

The leaves whisper jokes, and tease the air,
As mushrooms giggle without a care.
In this garden of quirks where laughter grows,
I stumble on humor that nature knows.

Gentle Touch of the Forest Floor

The soft earth tickles my wandering toes,
As curious critters peek from their rows.
I'm a guest in a land that's silly and bright,
Where frogs perform under the pale moonlight.

Each step's a dance with enchanted cheer,
While ants hold shows we can't all hear.
In this carpet of laughter, I lose my way,
As roots act as shoelaces, come what may.

Lost in Emerald Depths

Wrapped in green, with secrets to share,
Where capricious vines twine in midair.
I trip and tumble, falling for glee,
As the weeds join in—ah, welcome me!

A troll under bridges made of moss,
Jests about troubles, and I'm at a loss.
With fireflies acting as cheerleaders bright,
I join their giggles and dance through the night.

Where the Wild Things Grow

In corners dark with shadowed glee,
Fungi frolic, wild and free.
They wear hats made of greenish fluff,
Poking fun, they've had enough!

A squirrel twirls in acorn hats,
While frogs debate with dancing spats.
"Why wear shoes?" a mossy sage sighs,
"When bare feet let your spirit rise!"

Upon a tree, a snail's parade,
Squeezing through each leaf cascade.
They'd rather slide than shuffle fast,
A sticky trail – oh, what a blast!

Where laughter echoes through the leaves,
Ticklish whispers make the eaves.
Let wild things giggle, joke, and spin,
For joy grows brightly from within!

A Gentle Slumber Awaits

A blanket soft, the earth's embrace,
Lulls weary hearts to a cozy place.
Bees snooze soundly, honey dreams,
Mirthful hush in sunlit beams.

A chipmunk yawns, then curls in tight,
His acorn stash, a sleepy sight.
Under leaves like fairy beds,
Nature hums, while all are fed.

Clouds float by in gentle tease,
While twigs and branches sway with ease.
"Shhh!" they say, "It's nap time, friend,"
Where time itself seems to suspend.

In cozy nooks, with laughter hidden,
Where nature's secrets are well ridden.
Slumber deep, like whispers sweet,
Awaits us all beneath our feet!

The Stillness Beneath Our Feet

A dance of ants in perfect line,
With tiny hats and a dash of wine.
They plot and plan with flair and style,
While mushrooms giggle all the while.

Leaves drop down like parties crash,
Covered roots feel every splash.
A worm in shades of emerald green,
Swears he's the most dapper seen!

The ground is filled with silly tales,
Of grand adventures, swaps, and trails.
"Oh! Watch your step!" a ladybug warns,
"Underfoot lie our merry scorns!"

In stillness hums a world in jest,
With creatures plotting every quest.
Underneath where giggles meet,
A kingdom thrives beneath our feet!

Nature's Subtle Compliments

A whisper sweet from leaves above,
Compliments sent with gentle love.
"Your shoes are bright, they make me grin!"
"Your hair's a nest – where do I begin?"

A flower winks at passing bees,
"Your buzz is music, if you please."
The trees applaud with rustling cheer,
While rocks chuckle, "We're solid here!"

Worms hold court in earthy gowns,
"Why wear frowns, when life's a clown?"
With roots that twist in playful tease,
They sing a tune to tickle trees.

Nature scores with fun-filled rhymes,
Where laughter grows and levity climbs.
In gentle whispers, compliments flow,
In every nook where giggles grow!

Translucent Stories in the Gloaming

In twilight's laugh, the shadows dance,
A squirrel shares secrets, given a chance.
"Why do trees wear so much green?"
"A wardrobe choice, the best you've seen!"

The fireflies flash a puzzling code,
While crickets chirp on their tiny road.
"Why do they sing at night, not day?"
"Because they can sleep while the sun makes hay!"

The brook giggles as it flows along,
Making friends with every croaking song.
"Why are you always in such a rush?"
"Because I'm on time for a fishy hush!"

In evening's embrace, we all unite,
With laughter echoing into the night.
"Tell me a tale, don't hold it back!"
"Just whisper to me, when the owls attack!"

The Heartbeat of the Woods

In the woods, where giggles hide,
Trees gossip low, with roots that bide.
"Why do you stand so tall and straight?"
"Because I've got a leaf for every fate!"

The mushrooms chuckle, oh so round,
Poking fun at ants that abound.
"Why such a rush?" asks one small cap,
"Got a picnic planned, right in this gap!"

A woodpecker drums a merry beat,
Sending echoes bouncing to our feet.
"Is he a bandleader in disguise?"
"Just a wannabe, with no good lies!"

Through laughter and tales, we find our way,
In the heartbeat of woods, we all play.
"Share a secret, whisper it nice,"
"Only if you promise, not to think twice!"

Past Lives in a Hidden Glade

In a quiet nook where the wild things are,
Old trees recall tales from near and far.
"What did you see when you were young?"
"A rainbow party where frogs have sung!"

The hedgehogs are arguing who should win,
"Did you see my dance? Wasn't it a spin?"
"Please! Your waltz was more like a roll,"
"Only because it's my cardio goal!"

The ferns recall when they were blooms,
"Do we miss the sun? Or just the fumes?"
"We were wild and fancy, oh how we flew,"
"But we fit better after morning dew!"

In this hidden glade, we reminisce,
As laughter and memories blend in bliss.
"Tell me your dream from long ago,"
"Just a frog prince, with a banjo to show!"

Nature's Blanket of Reflection

Upon the ground, a quilt so bright,
Patches of color, a cheerful sight.
"Is it a rug for critters to nap?"
"Only if they promise to take a map!"

The clouds above have much to say,
Pillow fights planned at the end of the day.
"Why do you float, so high and grand?"
"To avoid the ants, who've poorly planned!"

The breeze whispers jokes through rustling leaves,
"Why do trees wear such crafty sleeves?"
"To keep secrets safe from passing skiers,
And to play peek-a-boo with the forest peers!"

In nature's embrace, we giggle and play,
Wrapped in laughter, as night turns to day.
"Tell me a riddle, I'm all ears,"
"Why did the branch grow so many gears?"

Fragments of Solitude in the Woodlands

In the silence of trees, a squirrel does prance,
Chasing its tail in a goofy dance.
A deer wears a grin, twinkling bright eyes,
While mushrooms conspire in sticky disguise.

Frogs play the drums with a splash and a croak,
As branches tell secrets in laughter and joke.
Leaves shuffle in glee, whispering cheer,
The woods hold my thoughts, making them clear.

A snail takes a selfie, moves slow as a train,
With a grin that confesses life's simple refrain.
The wind gives a chuckle, tickling my nose,
As acorns drop softly where mischief bestows.

Alone in the green, I find humor anew,
As nature's folly plays in every hue.
Each fragment of solitude holds joy's sweet spell,
In this woodland world, all is quite well.

The Gentle Touch of Forgotten Paths

On paths once well-trodden, where laughter had been,
Wanders a raccoon with pie-smeared chin.
The shadows of yesteryear giggle and thrash,
As wildflowers bloom in a colorful splash.

Tangled in vines, the old bench does moan,
Where pigeons have claimed the forgotten throne.
A ladybug lands with an elegant flair,
Proclaiming, 'I'm royalty!' in the crisp air.

The path twists and turns like a rabbit's own jig,
As butterflies gossip, their whispers so big.
Each tree stands as witness to stories retold,
Swapping their secrets like treasures of old.

As laughter floats gently, a breeze hums along,
In the touch of these paths, nothing feels wrong.
With each silly step, I embrace every laugh,
In the gentle embrace of the wild,

Whispers of Green Shadows

Shadowy whispers from branches above,
Tell tales of the critters who fell out of love.
The shy little hedgehog rolled up tight as a ball,
While twigs crack a joke that makes no sense at all.

A chubby chipmunk with cheeks full of snacks,
Juggles some acorns, balancing on tracks.
The fern nods in rhythm, with a laugh in the breeze,
As laughter erupts from the tiny green leaves.

The shadows all dance, doing waltzes and skips,
While ants form a train with a line of small trips.
They're headed to nowhere, but oh what a sight,
In the wondrous green shadows, everything feels right.

So let's join the fun in this giggly retreat,
Where each whisper brings joy with a skip in our feet.
In the embrace of these shadows, we twirl and we spin,
With every small chuckle, new adventures begin.

Lichen Dreams at Dusk

At dusk, the world glimmers with sparkles so bright,
    As lichen on rocks dons its shimmery light.
    Frogs wear pajamas, prepared for the night,
        While fireflies dance, a curious sight.

    The breeze tells the crickets a series of jokes,
    While owls laugh softly at their funny folks.
    A snail in a top hat takes a stroll with flair,
    As shadows indulge in their games of despair.

The moss whispers stories of days long since past,
    Of mushrooms that pirouette, merry and fast.
    In laughter, the forest engages with dreams,
While stars peek through branches, or so it seems.

So let's all join in for this whimsical play,
    Where lichen and laughter combine in the fray.
As night drapes its cloak, stars twinkle and gleam,
    In this humorous world, everything's a dream.

Embedded in Echoes of the Earth

Underneath the trees, a secret place,
Where whispers chuckle in a leafy space.
Rabbits hold meetings, wearing their hats,
While raccoons debate over sly little chats.

The roots of gossip grow deeper each day,
As fungi share lunch and join in the play.
A snail takes the stage, a diva so bold,
With stories of journeys from old to gold.

Squirrels laugh hard at the woes of the birds,
While worms write novels without any words.
Laughter erupts with each tickling breeze,
Nature's own comedy, designed to please.

So dance with the shadows, let giggles unfurl,
For life in the green wraps a whimsical twirl.
In the heart of the earth, a statewide jest,
Embedded in laughter, the earth's merry guest.

The Language of Mossy Reveries

In the realm of green, where dreams often sprout,
Mosses hold meetings, with hushes about.
Each tuft is a tale, spun soft like a quilt,
Whispering secrets, half-giggled, half-built.

The rocks wear their coats of a fuzzy delight,
While frogs tell the jokes that keep croaking all night.
A bug on a leaf gets the crowd in a roar,
As ants choreograph dances on forest floor.

Raccoons steal laughs from the owls, who stare,
While the wise old toad gives them quite the glare.
Every bright mushroom has jokes up its sleeve,
In a land where nonsense you'll surely believe.

So when you walk through where the green critters play,
Just listen for giggles that flutter and sway.
In journeys of laughter, our hearts take a seat,
In this earthly theater, where silly's a treat.

Verdant Hues of Forgotten Tales

In the shade of the pines, where laughter is free,
Plants share their plots, like it's gossip for tea.
Each leaf tells a story, with twists and with turns,
Of friendships and feasts and what each one learns.

The dandelions chuckle, with their fluffy heads,
As bees buzz along with the whispers that spread.
A butterfly flutters with grace and with flair,
Spreading wild giggles in the sun-kissed air.

Beneath all the growth, there's a dance on the floor,
With critters who waltz past the moss-laden door.
Life's vivid tales in shades of vibrant green,
Spun from the fibers of all that is seen.

So walk through the wild where the funny things nest,
In the verdant hues where humor's a quest.
Nature's own palette, with colors so bright,
Drips laughter like honey, delighting the night.

Growth in the Quiet Cracks

In the cracks of the pavement, where wildflowers bloom,
A joke-telling pebble brings laughter and zoom.
Each tiny sprout giggles, so bold and so small,
Sprinkling chuckles on concrete and all.

Like nature's own jesters, they quietly tease,
While ants in their suits march with elegant ease.
Caterpillars plot, and the gnarly old bees,
Share tales of lost socks in the quiet, sweet breeze.

A patch of green carpet lays low on the ground,
Where laughter and joy in each crevice is found.
The stones hold their breath as the ruckus unfolds,
Even weeds, with their humor, break out from the molds.

So look to the cracks where the laughter takes root,
In the stems of the grass, hear the jokes that are cute.
In the quiet of nature, there's always a jest,
Where growth meets the giggles, and life loves its best.

Conversations with the Ground Beneath

I whispered to the gravel, oh so sly,
It giggled back, "I'm just a rock, oh my!"
The earth chuckled low, with roots in the chat,
"Don't mind the worms, they just love to scatter!"

The daisies danced, twirling in the breeze,
"Hey there, dirt! Your makeup's a tease!"
The clovers chimed in, with a laugh quite loud,
"Let's throw a party, invite the whole crowd!"

The ants held a meeting, discussing their plans,
"Can we recruit squirrels, with dance moves so grand?"
The soil rolled its eyes, as if it could sigh,
"Don't invite the weeds, they always just pry!"

With roots intertwined, they plotted away,
A gathering of giggles to brighten the day!
The earth turned a shade of jolly old green,
As fun-loving critters made quite the scene!

Dreams Intertwined with Nature's Canvas

In the realm where petals dream of the sun,
A butterfly giggles, "Let's have some fun!"
The clouds paint their thoughts, whimsical and bright,
While pebbles chat softly, 'What a glorious sight!'

The grass giggles low, as it tickles the feet,
"Dance with me here, let's make life a treat!"
A nightingale chirps with a rhythm divine,
While shadows do waltzes, tiptoeing in line!

A squirrel in a bowtie, quite dapper, and spry,
Keeps stealing the acorns, oh my, oh my!
The dreams in the soil start to twinkle and glow,
As laughter erupts from the roots down below!

The leaves join the chorus, a rustling cheer,
"Who knew that the soil could be such a dear?"
A picture of joy, nature's canvas alive,
In the dance of the dreamers, we all can thrive!

The Ecosystem of Forgotten Thoughts

In a thicket of whispers where secrets retreat,
Lies a jumble of thoughts with a humorous beat.
The moss softly giggles, tickling the rocks,
"Remember that time we all lost our socks?"

A dandelion puff made a wish in jest,
"To float off and travel, what a fun quest!"
But bees buzzed along with their work in a dance,
"Forget the wish, come join us for a chance!"

Amidst tangled roots where old ideas nest,
A thought got distracted, forgot all the rest.
"To sing or to frolic? Ah, what should we do?"
The ferns simply replied, "How 'bout a stew?"

So the laughter erupted, a cacophony bright,
In the ecosystem of nonsense, delight!
Nature's sweet jests weave a colorful thread,
Where forgotten thoughts bloom and joyousness spread!

A Hug from the Earth

In the warmth of the soil, a cuddle so sweet,
"Welcome," it whispers, "rest your tired feet!"
The daisies lean in, with petals so wide,
"Join our cozy circle, come sit by our side!"

The toads croak a tune as frogs keep the beat,
With laughter and songs, oh what a treat!
A hug from the earth wraps 'round each small critter,
"Life's better together, not just in the litter!"

The trees throw a party, their branches all sway,
"To the rhythm of nature, come dance and play!"
With roots all entwined, they share tales of glee,
"Here's to our friendships, forever carefree!"

So when you feel low, just find a nice patch,
The earth will embrace you, a loving match!
A hug from the ground, so squishy and warm,
In the heart of the wild, it's a safe, happy swarm!

Secrets of a Shaded Grove

In a grove where whispers grow,
Squirrels plot with nuts in tow.
Trees wear hats of leafy green,
They gossip about the unseen.

Turtles on a log just lounge,
In their minds, they make a scrounge.
The shadows wink with leafy grins,
While light decides where the fun begins.

A raccoon juggles acorns high,
Underneath a laughing sky.
The sun hides, but giggles peek,
As branches sway in hide-and-seek.

So come and dance with woodland folks,
Where every tree has funny jokes.
In this shade, let laughter thrive,
With nature's quirks, we're all alive.

Thoughts Grown Wild

In the thicket, thoughts take flight,
Bunnies ponder wrong and right.
Frogs debate with rippling glee,
Should they croak or sing like me?

A butterfly pulls on its shades,
Complains about yesterday's raids.
Vines in knots sharing tales,
Of hasty hares and slow snails.

Sunbeams laugh as they descend,
They tickle leaves, their radiant friend.
Accorns plan a acorn ball,
With every critter invited, a free-for-all!

And in this chaos, joy erupt,
As nature's punchlines all corrupt.
So let your fancies grow like weeds,
In this wild land where laughter breeds.

The Forest's Quiet Journal

Beneath the canopy, secrets weave,
Bugs doodle in their art naive.
A ladybug writes quite a tale,
Of missing socks and scented trail.

The wind whispers puns to the trees,
While branches snort with leafy wheeze.
A breeze carries giggles like a song,
In this diary, where we all belong.

Mushrooms hold an open chat,
About the squirrel who wears a hat.
They laugh at tales of silly sprout,
And wonder when the rain will shout.

In the ink of dusk, stories sprout,
With every shadow casting doubt.
So listen well, oh woodland kin,
For in this journal, life begins.

Echoes in the Underbrush

Rustling leaves, a hidden song,
Where critters laugh all day long.
A hedgehog rolls a story tight,
While fireflies flash their merry light.

In the underbrush, secrets hum,
As ants march to a goofy drum.
Weeds waltz with the startled fawn,
In the twilight, dusk yawns on and on.

The mushrooms hold a midnight feast,
With fairy tales and jokes unleashed.
A warbler tells of tallest trees,
While dancing leaves shout, "Can't you see?"

So join the fun where echoes play,
In this wild spot where we sway.
With laughter sprung from every nook,
The forest's heart is one big book.

Secrets in the Forest's Fold

In quiet woods, the whispers creep,
Where shadows dance and secrets sleep.
A squirrel laughs, all nuts in tow,
While trees gossip in breezy flow.

The mushrooms wear their polka dots,
As rabbits race in silly spots.
A wise old owl with crooked glasses,
Winks at the world, as laughter passes.

Pinecones tumble down with glee,
While ants debate a life of tea.
A frog, in jest, jumps on a log,
And croaks his verse—a comic frog!

Beneath the ferns, a turtle grins,
Sipping dew like it's fine gin.
In this fold of laughter hidden,
Nature's quirks are rarely bidden.

A Tapestry of Time and Texture

The bark of trees—rough stitching seams,
Weaving together our wildest dreams.
With knots and tangles, stories spun,
Life's silly tales have just begun.

The leaves, like feathers, float and sway,
In a breeze that tickles all the way.
A chipmunk squeaks a funny rhyme,
While mossy carpets stretch through time.

Curly vines, they're nature's hair,
Braided up without a care.
A squirrel's twirl, a dandelion's twist,
This forest stage—none can resist!

Old stones chuckle, their tales unfold,
Of moments shared, both brave and bold.
In this patchwork of green delight,
Nature's comic relief takes flight.

Lichen's Lament on Ancient Stones

Upon a rock, so wise and gray,
The lichen sighs, 'Oh what a day!'
A puff of wind disrupts its peace,
'Just let me chill, give me release!'

With every raindrop, it sighs aloud,
'Oh, why must you be so very proud?'
'Your beauty fades, while I stay still,
A quirky patch of greenish thrill.'

Snails inch by with graceful flair,
While crickets share their songs in the air.
The sun beams down, a cheeky light,
As lichen mocks, 'This isn't right!'

Yet still it clings, a loyal friend,
To those old stones that seem to bend.
In humor's grasp, they share their tale,
Of patience found beneath the veil.

Dewdrops and Dappled Light

The morning breaks with a dewy grin,
As sunlight tickles, and day begins.
Each drop a diamond, a wink of glee,
As bees buzz by, in harmony.

The shadows stretch like yawning cats,
While rabbits hop in dapper hats.
A ladybug, on a leaf so bright,
Disputes the matter of left or right.

With twinkling eyes, the fern unfolds,
While stories of chaos quietly told.
A dragonfly zooms on a silly slip,
Just dodging a plant's playful grip.

In dappled light, the forest laughs,
While childhood echoes in nature's halves.
With each new dawn, the fun ignites,
In a swirl of colors and frolics bright.

Where the Old Roots Whisper

In the garden where secrets twine,
Old roots gossip, sipping sunshine.
They chuckle softly, tales they weave,
Of socks lost under leaves, I believe.

A worm winks with a mischievous grin,
Teasing moles for their shifty kin.
The daisies nod, they're in on the fun,
While crickets chirp, their laughter begun.

The ants parade with tiny hats,
Underneath a tree, a party chats.
A squirrel juggles acorns in a rush,
While mushrooms squabble, "Hush, little tush!"

As birds chirp jokes from branches high,
The old roots stretch, let out a sigh.
"Life is rich and often absurd,
Just share a laugh — spread the word!"

Soft Steps Through Liquid Green

Splash, splash, the puddles gleam,
Waddling frogs in a liquid dream.
With each leap, they croak a tune,
Dancing under a grinning moon.

The grass tickles as I wander by,
With each step, a giggle in the sky.
The flowers gossip in vibrant hues,
Swapping tales of their morning snooze.

A snail slides in, all slow and grand,
With aspirations to join the band.
"Just gimme a beat, I'll show you how,
To rap about this lovely brown cow!"

As bugs do the two-step on the leaf,
Their tiny feet show no sign of grief.
While raindrops form a sparkling crown,
The trees sway, laughing their leafy frown.

Stories Woven in Earth's Fabric

Underfoot, tales twist and twine,
Each step holds laughter and divine.
Rabbits share rights to the fluffiest burrow,
While ants discuss their colony's thorough.

Beetles boast of shiny backs,
Competitions held on the grassy tracks.
Seeds gossip of where they'll take flight,
Past the daffodils that wave goodnight.

Earthworms write poems deep down low,
With ink of muddy water flow.
Squirrels architect a nutty quest,
Claiming victory at every jest.

In this rich land of humble glee,
Nature's song is like a spree.
So join the chorus, bring your cheer,
For under the surface, laughter is clear!

The Poetry of Slow Embrace

In a world that spins too fast,
Embrace the sloth; glance, don't blast.
With a grin, it invites you near,
To marvel at life's hum, oh dear!

The clouds float by, quite unsure,
"Is it time for a nap or a fun little tour?"
A lazy breeze whispers to the trees,
"Let's write a sonnet, just with ease."

Each flower sways in a shuffled dance,
Hoping for love's confused romance.
"Tomorrow we'll bloom, but today let's play,
As sunlight bathes us in a golden ray."

And so we chuckle in this quaint ballet,
Slow moments matter, come what may.
Dance with the daisies, relish the haze,
In this funny waltz, let's bask and blaze!

Between Stone and Soil

In the cracks where laughter hides,
A worm jokes with a pebble's pride.
Grass tickles those who sit too low,
While ants wear hats made of a crow.

Sunshine dances, tricks on rocks,
While shadows play with silly socks.
Nature's jester hides in green,
With giggles that we've never seen.

The stone forgets its sturdy past,
As flowers tease with scents so vast.
Here in between, the fun's afoot,
With grinning daisies at the root.

So lift your gaze and let it slide,
Where soil and slapstick coincide.
In nature's jest, we find our way,
With chuckles marking every day.

The Sigh of the Old Tree

The old tree leans, it's heard the tales,
Of squirrels dressed up in tiny veils.
With branches bent from years of glee,
It whispers jokes from bark to leaf.

A fox once tried to climb so high,
But slipped and fell, oh my, oh my!
The laughter echoed far and wide,
As the old tree chuckled deep inside.

With roots that wiggle beneath the ground,
And leaves that sway to a funny sound,
The sigh it gives, a hearty cheer,
For every giggle that it can hear.

So if you pass beneath this sage,
Join in the humor of its age.
For wisdom comes with mirth, you see,
In every crack of that old tree.

Moss-Covered Remnants

On ancient stones where laughter blooms,
A gnome appears in funny costumes.
With moss for hair and rocks for shoes,
He dances unaware of the news.

Old bricks blush with emerald green,
Telling stories we've never seen.
A giggle here, a chuckle there,
In every nook, humor's in the air.

The walls hold secrets, textures bold,
Of critters who've outsmarted the cold.
A snail's slow crawl, a turtle's plight,
Become the punchlines in the night.

So lift a toast to what remains,
The funny tales in nature's veins.
Where moss softens the edge of age,
And humor whispers from every page.

The Weight of the World

A boulder sits, it takes a seat,
While ants bring snacks and dance on feet.
"Oh, what a load!" the stone will sigh,
"I can't believe I'm stuck here high!"

Clouds parade like fluffy jesters,
Mocking leaves with ticklish gestures.
Each gust of wind, a playful shove,
As blooms erupt in fits of love.

The world spins round with silly schemes,
As dandelions plot in dreams.
"Lighten up!" a flower shouts,
With petals flapping, casting doubts.

So let the rocks and roots conspire,
In nature's mix of light and fire.
With laughter lifting heavy loads,
Our joys sprout wild in winding roads.

Lightened

A breeze sweeps through with jokes to share,
While flowers giggle in the warm air.
Old twigs dance like musicians grand,
With whispers from the forest band.

A leaf once slipped on dew so clear,
And tumbled down, oh what a cheer!
It landed soft on mossy beds,
Where dreams and humor weave their threads.

The sun's bright rays, a playful tease,
Make shadows laugh among the trees.
With roots that wriggle, 'round they leap,
Creating mischief, not a peep.

So join the dance, lift off your weight,
And let the world be your best mate.
In every laugh, the heart will find,
A lighter way to unwind.

A Symphony of Fungi and Ferns

In the forest's lively choir,
Mushrooms dance with roots like wires.
Ferns sway gently with a grin,
While fairies giggle through the din.

Toadstools wear their polka dots,
Crickets play their tiny flops.
Each sprout shares a silly tale,
A whimsical, wild woodland trail.

Squirrels leap from tree to tree,
Chasing shadows just for glee.
Laughter hangs on every breeze,
Nature's jest is sure to please.

So grab your cheer and join the jest,
In this green patch where life is best.
With every step, a giggle blooms,
In this green world, there's no room for glooms.

Beneath the Green Veil

Underneath the leafy cloak,
Lies a world that loves to poke.
Tiny bugs in bowler hats,
Debate with worms on comfy mats.

Liverworts wear their silken shoes,
While beetles brag about their views.
Beneath the green, it's quite the scene,
A comedy of nature's routine.

Giggles bubble in the brook,
With fish that read from funny books.
Each ripple laughs with a small splash,
As frogs leap in with a great big crash.

So lift the veil and take a peek,
At whimsy where the garden speaks.
With every twist and green delight,
Funny stories take flight in sight.

Echoes of Innocence in the Moss

In the soft green carpet below,
Whispers share what they know.
That ladybugs with tiny pals,
Once held council with the gales.

Beneath the weight of twigs and leaves,
A troupe of ants in fun reprieves.
They march in lines, a funny clatter,
Creating joy in tiny patter.

Crickets tune their evening songs,
While raccoons plan their nightly throngs.
In this mossy realm of playful cheer,
Laughter echoes, crystal clear.

So listen close to nature's play,
In shadows where the giggles sway.
A symphony of simple joy,
Echoes of innocence won't annoy.

The Poetry of Forgotten Paths

On paths where the sunlight weaves,
Old tales hang on whispering leaves.
A gnome with socks that barely match,
Mumbles secrets from a scratch.

Once tripped a toad on a muddy part,
Who claimed he had a poet's heart.
His verses were made of hops and leaps,
And left behind a trail of peeps.

With every turn, a chuckle grows,
Where wildflowers run in rows.
Every stone and fern has got a say,
In the poetry of this playful way.

So wander forth on paths long lost,
Laughing gladly at any cost.
In tangled roots and playful grass,
Life's silly script invites us to pass.

www.ingramcontent.com/pod-product-compliance
Lightning Source LLC
Chambersburg PA
CBHW071828160426
43209CB00003B/243